SECRETS OF
WINNING PEOPLE

J. DONALD WALTERS

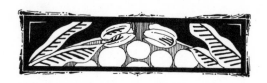

Hardbound edition, first printing 1993

Copyright 1993
J. Donald Walters

Text Illustrations: Karen White

Illustrations copyright 1993
Crystal Clarity, Publishers

ISBN 1-56589-030-2

10 9 8 7 6 5 4 3 2 1

PRINTED IN HONG KONG

Crystal Clarity
P U B L I S H E R S

14618 Tyler Foote Road, Nevada City, CA 95959
1 (800) 424-1055

A seed thought is offered for every day of the month. Begin a day at the appropriate date. Repeat the saying several times: first out loud, then softly, then in a whisper, and then only mentally. With each repetition, allow the words to become absorbed ever more deeply into your subconscious. Thus, gradually, you will acquire as complete an understanding as one might gain from a year's course in the subject. At this point, indeed, the truths set forth here will have become your own.

Keep the book open at the pertinent page throughout the day. Refer to it occasionally during moments of leisure. Relate the saying as often as possible to real situations in your life.

Then at night, before you go to bed, repeat the thought several times more. While falling asleep, carry the words into your subconscious, absorbing their positive influence into your whole being. Let it become thereby an integral part of your normal consciousness.

DAY

1

THE SECRET OF

WINNING PEOPLE

IS....

to be deeply convinced, first,

of the truth of your proposal.

DAY

2

THE SECRET OF

WINNING PEOPLE

IS....

enthusiasm for the truth as

you perceive it.

DAY

3

THE SECRET OF
WINNING PEOPLE

IS....

never telling an untruth, but

letting sincerity take such

deep root within you that your

simple word carries conviction.

DAY

4

THE SECRET OF

WINNING PEOPLE

IS....

addressing the issues calmly,

never emotionally or excitedly.

To put it otherwise: When

trying to persuade someone,

use adjectives sparingly.

DAY

5

THE SECRET OF
WINNING PEOPLE
IS....

creating a relaxed

atmosphere, for tension

induces resistance to new

ideas, whereas relaxation

fosters receptivity.

DAY

6

THE SECRET OF
WINNING PEOPLE
IS....

to present points of mutual
agreement before proceeding
to your central theme.

DAY

7

THE SECRET OF

WINNING PEOPLE

IS....

to remain calm under attack,

and withhold recognition from

comments that are made

simply to offend.

DAY

8

THE SECRET OF

WINNING PEOPLE

IS....

to be convinced that the other

person, too, wants to arrive

at the truth.

DAY
9

THE SECRET OF

WINNING PEOPLE

IS....

desiring that the truth prevail,

and being willing to change

your mind instantly, should

the facts of a matter prove

you wrong.

DAY
10

THE SECRET OF
WINNING PEOPLE
IS....

seeing yourself as the other

person's friend and well-wisher.

DAY

11

THE SECRET OF
WINNING PEOPLE
IS....

putting yourself in the other
person's shoes; considering
his point of view (whether or
not you refer to it) before you
present your own.

DAY

12

THE SECRET OF
WINNING PEOPLE
IS....

concentrating on the other

person's needs, not your own.

DAY

13

THE SECRET OF

WINNING PEOPLE

IS....

under-emphasizing the

pronoun, "I."

DAY

14

THE SECRET OF
WINNING PEOPLE
IS....

appealing to a person's

altruism; convincing him of

the universal benefits

of your proposal.

DAY

15

THE SECRET OF
WINNING PEOPLE
IS....

to refrain from making leaps

of logic for which your

listeners are not prepared.

16

THE SECRET OF
WINNING PEOPLE
IS....

having the patience to let
others come to your position
in their own time. (Reflect, it
probably took *you* time, too,
to arrive there.)

DAY

17

THE SECRET OF
WINNING PEOPLE
IS....

responsiveness to

alternative suggestions.

DAY

18

THE SECRET OF

WINNING PEOPLE

IS....

helping a person to convince

himself, and not overwhelming

him with your enthusiasm.

DAY

19

THE SECRET OF
WINNING PEOPLE
IS....

to enter into your subject
wholeheartedly, with full
concentration; making your
every word count.

D A Y
20

THE SECRET OF
WINNING PEOPLE
IS....

creativity and spontaneity;

not holding fixedly to anything

you've prepared to say.

THE SECRET OF
WINNING PEOPLE
IS....

magnetism; projecting

your convictions with

equivalent energy.

DAY

22

THE SECRET OF

WINNING PEOPLE

IS....

never to accept a defensive
position. If attacked for your
ideas, counter good-humoredly,
but with conviction. Never
make excuses for anything in
which you sincerely believe.

THE SECRET OF

WINNING PEOPLE

IS....

never belittling the opinions,

however uninformed, of those

whom you are seeking

to convince.

THE SECRET OF

WINNING PEOPLE

IS....

not pleading, to your listener's

disadvantage, your own

greater knowledge or

experience, but letting crystal

clarity be your sole defense.

DAY

25

THE SECRET OF

WINNING PEOPLE

IS....

to support your statements

with qualified evidence, and

avoid such vague claims as,

"Lots of people say so."

DAY

26

THE SECRET OF

WINNING PEOPLE

IS....

to keep the discussion as

closely to the issues

as possible.

DAY
27

THE SECRET OF

WINNING PEOPLE

IS....

to concentrate on presenting

solutions, and not diminish

the energy of your

presentation by dwelling

lengthily on the problems.

DAY
28

THE SECRET OF
WINNING PEOPLE
IS....

to introduce your point early,

and not keep your listeners in

suspense, lest tension build

up within them, making them

resistant to your ideas.

DAY

29

THE SECRET OF
WINNING PEOPLE
IS....

in any difference of opinion, to

look for points of agreement,

and not resort to criticism

or accusation.

D A Y

30

THE SECRET OF
WINNING PEOPLE
IS....

not concealing counter-

arguments, but presenting

them fairly, then placing

them in the context of a

broader truth.

DAY

31

THE SECRET OF
WINNING PEOPLE
IS....

forging lasting, not brittle,

bonds with people, lest, even

in victory, you lose their

esteem and loyalty.

Other Books in the **Secrets** Series
by J. Donald Walters

Secrets of Happiness

Secrets of Friendship

Secrets of Love

Secrets of Inner Peace

Secrets of Success

Secrets for Men

Secrets for Women

Secrets of Prosperity

Secrets of Leadership

Secrets of Self-Acceptance

Secrets of Radiant Health and Well-Being

Secrets of Bringing Peace on Earth

Design: Sara Cryer
Illustrations: Karen White
Typesetting: Robert Froelick
Photography: Mark McGinnis